My Heart Remembers

MY HEART REMEMBERS

poems by Dorothy Johnson

Haley's

Athol, Massachusetts

Haley's
488 South Main Street
Athol, MA 01331
haley.antique@verizon.net • 978.249.9400

Copy edited by Ellen Woodbury.

Cover photo by Dale Monette.

Library of Congress Cataloging-in-Publication Data
Names: Johnson, Dorothy, 1933- author.
Title: My heart remembers / poems by Dorothy Johnson.
Description: Athol, Massachusetts : Haley's, [2021] | Summary: "a
   collection of recent poems by the playwright Dorothy Johnson"--
Provided
   by publisher.
Identifiers: LCCN 2021033518 (print) | LCCN 2021033519
(ebook) | ISBN
   9781948380461 (hardback) | ISBN 9781948380454 (paperback)
| ISBN
   9781948380478 (adobe pdf)
Subjects: LCGFT: Poetry.
Classification: LCC PS3610.O3385 M9 2021 (print) | LCC
PS3610.O3385
   (ebook) | DDC 811/.6--dc23
LC record available at https://lccn.loc.gov/2021033518
LC ebook record available at https://lccn.loc.gov/2021033519

THEY TOUCHED MY HEART
a dedication

They touched my heart,
those doctors
at the UMass Medical Center
in Worcester,
when they pushed a leaky valve
to one side
and placed a new one there.
It was from an animal.
I'm grateful
to those doctors and nurses,
to the animal,
and to the researchers
who took this process
from an experiment
to an ordinary procedure.
Without them
I would not have had
more years
to spend with loving friends,
with books, and with the telephone
all during the pandemic
and with Zoom meetings.
There would have been no poems,
no book, no further joy.
I am grateful for all.

KINDNESS
an epigraph

My heart remembers
kindnesses,
many from strangers,
many from friends.
Such simple gifts
have untold value
equally good to give
as to receive.

Contents

PERSONAL

A SLY MAGICIAN CONJURING
a foreword by Anna Mundow

"If poetry comes not as naturally as leaves to a tree, it had better not come at all," John Keats declares in a letter to a friend in 1818. And Dorothy Johnson, writing a little over two hundred years later, has reached the same conclusion.

"I cannot force a poem/like an amaryllis/in a pot . . . ," she observes in one of the many gems that make up this collection. A stray thought or memory, a change in the weather, a recent death, an ancient myth—any one of them may alight like a bird at her backyard feeder, demanding attention and sparking her imagination. Then, gradually and mysteriously, her "moment of vision," as another English poet once described it, becomes something that we, too, can see and feel.

Some of the poems here are like good jokes. They take us by surprise—ever thought about gravity and . . . gravy? Others touch the heart, as Dorothy, in her dedication, imagines cardiac surgeons doing when they replaced her leaky valve. Still others capture the anxieties and absurdities of our current times. But thanks to Dorothy's light touch—which has been perfected over a lifetime of reading and writing—the overall effect, whatever the subject, is delightful.

As you read, you may feel as though you have been welcomed into her kitchen where a variety of objects, some whimsical, some elegant, catch the eye. Then you realize that somehow all four seasons of the New England year along with a handful of ancestors and an assortment of Greek gods has materialized at the table. This sly magician has conjured them all—and more—out of thin air. And what a feast it is.

OBSERVATIONS AND OPINIONS

QUESTIONS

How do we know
who is one of us?
Must we use
the same language,
the same clichés,
sing the same songs?
Do we dare
to step outside
the line we've drawn?
What are we afraid of?
That we'll discover
we are one of them?
What will that do to us?

LANGUAGE

Language shifts.
Who can remember
when receipt became recipe
or forsooth became in truth
or even honestly?
Someone must know when F became S in print.
Words and letters turn aside
and hide in shifting sands.
When the sands shift again
which archaic words
will slip into the sea
to be lost forever?

HEROES

How does a sandwich
get called a hero?
Consider a different spelling
in a different language
that sounds familiar.
You might say
a gyro became a hero
by satisfying a hunger.
No. I doubt any sandwich
can truly be heroic.
We hear of heroes in wartime.
Brave heroes live and die
in bloody conflict,
but war alone does not
make a hero.
We also talk of heroes
when people do extraordinary things
in time of crisis,
but I think anybody
in this life
of ordinary highs and lows
who shows love of others throughout—
well, that's a hero to me.

ENDS

The ocean seems to me to have no end.
Waves continuously beat against the shore.
Movement is constant.
Though I cannot see the fish
or things that grow along the sea beds
I know they're there.
There's no beginning and no end
as far as I can see.
I much prefer things
with beginnings, middles, and ends
like human beings,
stories, plays, and seasons.
Curtains go up and curtains come down
all neat and satisfying.
You know where you are
when things have beginnings
and middles and ends.

FAITH

What faith it must take
to be a dancer,
to leap into the air so free,
to be beautiful,
and to know you will come down safe
or be rescued by strong arms
still above the earth.
I know that they must fall
sometimes and get up to leap again
over and over.
It's how they learn their skills,
where they learn their faith.

JUSTIFICATION

Lions never justify taking an antelope.
Why should they?

Look at what we have taken:
land—forests and rivers
to create cities and swimming pools,
coal mines and oil fields,
churches and yards with fences,
and keep-out signs.

We've even taken lions themselves—
for zoos and circuses and trophies
or even worse, for pets
declawed and defanged.

Where's our justification?

GAINS AND LOSSES

Sometimes I think
so much has changed
just in my lifetime alone
it feels as if the earth is shifting.
What have we gained
in all that time?
Much that is useful, much good, and much concerning.
Think cell phones, computers, plastics of every kind,
shopping malls, legal pot, agribusiness, climate change,
twelve-step programs, fashionable denim, for-profit prisons,
new viruses, the CIA, our and others' racism,
and an army always at some war somewhere.
Then, too, what have we lost?
Telephone books with yellow pages,
penmanship, too much of the rain forest,
pay phones, polio, privacy, and our innocence.
No longer can we think we are special,
safe from attack, nor can we think
that all of us are safe
on our streets and in our homes.
Technology is growing every day
but wisdom lags far, far behind.

NEEDS

What do we really need?
The basics are
food, shelter, sleep, air,
and sun to warm our bones
and give us light,
though nothing's guaranteed.
I'm sure there's more,
but these seem to be enough for now.
If you consider
our homes are borrowed
from those who follow us,
then you have to know
entitlements are few
and very simple.
Of course, if you believe
that we're supposed to have
all that and more,
as if we're here for all time,
as if we have somehow
deserved it—
then that's another story.

WHITE PRIVILEGE

The assumption has been
that Americans are white and Christian.
Look at our history.
From the beginning,
we did not take kindly
to differences.
I understate the case.
We brutalized, enslaved,
and drove them off their land.
When others came
with other languages,
we kept them at a distance
even though they were white.
We may have needed their labor,
but they were different.
And now after centuries,
we try to maintain our privilege
by taking it for granted.

MORE OR LESS

Do fewer people have less wisdom?
Maybe it's the other way around,
and more people have less wisdom.
I think not.
Though it grates on my ear,
it seems we're losing fewer
and using less instead.
Our language is changing.
Usage used to be sure.
Rules were rules,
but these days, less is more,
and fewer disappearing
except for the fussy few.

PRIVILEGE

It feels like everyday,
not like privilege,
the right to walk
freely anywhere,
to work with
a sense of accomplishment,
to take for granted
my home will be there
when I am out and come home
and that I will have a home
where I can sleep
safely in my bed at night.
It does not feel
like privilege,
and yet I know it must be,
for I can see
too many others
who cannot share it.

LOVE

How do I describe love?
I don't mean passion
or being in love.
They have needs all their own.
No, something gentler
like the scent of lilacs in the air.
It makes you want to be better,
kinder, more generous,
and likely to risk letting
yourself be known and to know others
and even more, to be at one
with the scent of lilacs in the air.

OWNERS OF BOOKS

Others have owned
the books I own.
Often they write their names
on the flyleaf,
and sometimes they leave
notes in the margins
for words that seemed important.
Also they've bought things and leave the receipts
which they've used as bookmarks.
Recently, I opened an old copy
of *The Bridge over San Luis Rey*
signed by Thornton Wilder
to Zella Pianarosa,
Pittsfield, August 1939.
I wonder who she was,
that woman with the beautiful name.
I hope she liked the book
and we had that in common.

BOOKS

Only with certain friends
can I gossip about books.
About who said what
and why they took
one action or another.
Or to complain
about the books themselves.
No longer are the signatures
(a curious word unrelated
to names on checks or documents)
sewed but glued
against the spines.
As the glue dries out
the book can split apart.
It seems that modern books
aren't meant to stay on shelves
after they've been read
but are meant to be
devoured and digested
and then thrown away
like so much of modern life.

THE FATES

Yesterday
I read a line
that said it was absurd
to think that life
begins with birth,
because the pattern
had been set so long before.
Our genes determine
who we are.
Our fates are set.
We are a part
of all who ever were
from parents
who had parents.
on and on,
adding other genes
by marriage or whatever.
Our grandmothers
had themselves two grandmothers.
Did they ever think
the line could end with me,
or do the fates still
never mind?

ALL ROADS

If all roads lead to Rome,
it stands to reason
those same roads lead out.
We have to know
which way is forward.

AVERAGE PEOPLE
THEM AND US

Average people are not
average to themselves.
Neither are they
ordinary inside.
No, inside they're special.
It's just that life
has never called
on us to do
something grand.
Thus, we continue
with ordinary days,
but sometimes
we dream of special times
when we could do
extraordinary things
if called upon.

SHELTER

As we plodded through
the winter months,
the days went by
one by one,
and pages in our calendars
were turned at last
so we are closer to the sun
of April days and May's new buds.
There's joy in that achievement.
We've weathered storms
and cold dark days.
Winter gave us time to rest,
to find our pleasures warm within.
We've been sheltered,
but what of those
who have no home?
Where do our sisters and brothers sleep?
Who shelters them?

MODERN LIFE

Machines wash our clothes
and even our dishes now.
There are robots to vacuum our floors
and timers to start and stop our stoves.
What do we do
with the time we save
since our chores are made
so much easier?
How do we live in harmony
with the earth
when there are so many
roads and highways
splitting the countryside
for so many vehicles
in constant movement?
If there's an answer,
I don't know it.

WHO OWNS A TREE?

When you consider
how long it takes to grow,
it takes no time at all
to plant a tree.
Then you wait
and watch it year by year
shiver in a summer breeze
or withstand the winter snows
while slowly it adds
ring to ring and leaf to leaf
and becomes itself—
a tree that can't be owned
no matter who planted it
or on whose property it stands.
Even the property we think we own
can't be owned.
Not really.
We may use it for a lifetime
and keep the deeds to pass on.
Deeds are only paper, after all,
and soon other selves
will hold those papers
and think they own the land
and the tree you planted long before.

MUTABILITY

Everything changes.
Everything is mutable.
We seem to have forgotten the word,
though English poets used it—
Byron, Shelley, Wordsworth—
but we take change for granted,
thinking what is new is good.
Often it is,
like spring after a hard winter.
But often what is new
is like a gift with strings attached,
and only later
do we know the cost.

REMEMBERING
1964

Two black children, boy and girl,
burned to death
in the cabin provided for migrants
while their parents picked apples
in the Hudson Valley.
Some said the children
were playing with matches.
Perhaps they were.
The parents wept
as the children were buried
in the cold New York earth
without a stone or marker.
Their names were lost
long ago.
Is anyone else left
who remembers?

MARTIN LUTHER KING JR. DAY

Today I was reminded
of the day MLK was shot.
Then, I was in New Orleans
teaching freshmen in a federal program
at a traditionally black college.
When we heard the news,
my students sagged, then stood and declared
they would go to Atlanta.
Many did go. Still, the college
held a mournful assembly the next day.
On Sunday afternoon,
there was a rally in Jackson Square.
Every inch of the square was peopled,
black and white together.
Someone cried out, "There's a gun!"
But there was no gun—only fear.
All afternoon, the pigeons who lived there
had no place to rest.
Over and over,
any movement at all sent
a cloud of pigeons rushing upward
all blue and gray,
crowding the sky
while we, black and white together,
mourned in Jackson Square
and then we went
our separate ways
to our separate neighborhoods,
thinking we mourned a great man,
and we took his words to heart.

BOUNDARIES

Snow obscures boundaries.
I cannot tell where my land ends
and theirs begins.
How did it ever become ours and theirs?
Words on paper, registered in the county,
paid for by paper as work is paid.
How can land be owned this way?
We are here such a little while.
We make assumptions
as did the Wampanoags and the Nipmucs
when they hunted on this same land.
Of course, then land wasn't owned.
It was no more theirs than ours—
just borrowed for a little while.
Ah, well, snow melts,
and paper disintegrates eventually.

ENOUGH

How do we define enough?
Enough food, enough time, enough money—
how much is enough?
I once knew a Russian woman
who had been starved in World War II.
She worried about food. Was there enough?
I never knew if she meant for herself or for everybody.
Also I have a friend who seems never to have enough time.
She is always late. Too many things to do
in the little time she set for herself.
As for money, our world is ruled by it.
For some people there will never be enough.
Either they have to work for more
or steal it—legally or otherwise.
And others fear spending what they have.
What if they don't have enough left?
Some people will never be satisfied,
but most of us, if we honestly look at ourselves,
seem to have just enough contentment.

THE SEVEN SINS

The seven sins are deadly
because they make
servants of us all.
We do not choose
to lust or envy,
but we must.
Neither do we wish
to gourmandize
or find our heart's delight
in avarice,
but once we begin
and find ourselves upon that path,
if we are wise,
we'll turn away.
If not, we'll do
whatever sin demands.

THE MOON

This morning, I watched the moon set
slowly, slowly like a lady.
It seemed as if
she sat at the edge of a bed
and, because of a cloud,
she pulled the covers over her
so slowly, I wondered
what she was waiting for.
Then, on the other side
of my small world,
the sun began to send
the first gold along the horizon.
By the time the golden glow
showed its fire,
rising with the sun,
the moon was done.
She dimmed her light
and was gone.

INDIAN SUMMER

Is it a racist thing
to call them so,
those soft warm days
after a frost?
Long ago (for I am old),
in school I learned that these days
brought raids on settlements.
I also learned that settlers were good,
civilizing the land and bringing
their religion to Godless souls.
Native ways were pagan
and, thus, the devil's work.
I don't know what is taught now,
but I hope it's closer to the truth.
And I'll still call these days Indian Summer,
for they're a pleasant interlude
before we have to put on gloves
and button up our coats.

MOUNTAINS

I like New England mountains,
but to Westerners, they seem like puny hills.
It's all in your perspective.
When you are used to rolling grassy mounds,
a good-sized hill looks to be a mountain.
The others seem too big,
too huge to fit into a landscape.
To my eyes, they are so much,
they make me know my insignificance.
Oh, no. Not for me the Rockies.
I'll take Tom, Monadnock, Holyoke,
and all those Green and White ones.
For me, they are comfortable,
accessible, and like me,
they're right where they belong.

WHAT DO WE CALL IT?

Someone has made a new merry-go-round—
not really made but rebuilt an old
carnival ride as a sculpture.
The fancy has gone, stripped down to the bones
unpainted, sanded, and plain—
almost a ghost of a ride.
No music plays, and no children laugh
as the horses go round and round.
Memory can paint the horses
black and white and gray
with flashing eyes and scarlet reins
held tight in sticky hands.
But memory doesn't serve this art.
Instead, we look for truth,
for what is at the root,
but it still leaves us a question.
Can a merry-go-round
be a sculpture
without music, color, and light
and still be a merry-go-round?
One might ask
if a skeleton, articulated and
hung in an anatomy lab
became something else—
became what it is?
Is it no longer a man?

FANELLI'S CAROUSEL

To see the stripped-down
skeleton of a carousel
is to see a sculpture.
The bare wood and aluminum horses
tell of a past of painted glory.
White lights surround the outer rim.
Within, machinery makes the horses
rise and fall as if a child were riding,
but no happy laughter's heard.
Not here. Only memory evokes a vision
of days long gone and tuned to what is real.
The child's toy thing has become art.
There is truth here deep within
the roots of a reality
that stirs imagination.
Serious hands worked to strip the paint,
the past and present fused now into art.
It took imagination to see the crates
that held it stilled for years and years
and courage to make it live again.
And most of all, it took great love
to make the vision real.

EXTINCTION

Extinction is forever.
We let species after species
disappear, and most of us forget them,
but we also forget
that we are animals, too,
as we waste the earth's goodness with our wars and greed.
Earth can exist without us
just as it has always gone on
as species after species disappear.

GUNS

It is no child's game.
"Bang, bang. You're dead!"
Children fall,
but they get up again,
and everybody goes home safe.
It matters little
whether you are a man, woman, child,
husband, wife, sportsman,
or even if you wear a uniform.
When a gun is involved,
too often, people die.
They'll never again get up.
They'll never again go home.

TRUTH

I much prefer plain speech,
not fancy words that obfuscate
and make obscure all meaning.
Say what you will
and mean what you say
and speak an ordinary truth.
Truth itself is humdrum—
ordinary as a slice of bread—
not veneered with high-flown words.
Yet there are many kinds of bread,
so it may seem elusive.
What I seek is a daily bread,
a solid loaf with no pretension,
an honest loaf
we all can trust.
That should be the daily bread
we've sought so long.

COMPARISONS

If I am better than,
does that make you less than?
If I know more than you,
does that make me more valuable?
Why do we make these comparisons?
I cannot answer that.
I do know there's much
that I don't know,
and I know of many who know more,
so sometimes I wonder
who is sure of herself or himself?
Did Shakespeare compare himself to Marlowe
and Mozart himself to Salieri?
Unthinkable now,
but who has more value,
or was each enough in himself?
Perhaps all persons and poets compete,
even those we've made famous.
Yeats may have compared himself to John Donne
and Adrienne Rich to Emily Dickinson
or to John Donne as well.
Is anyone satisfied with a personal best?
Is it ever enough,
or will we always know
that there are those
who will do it better?

EVOLUTION

Evolution hasn't ended
with humans standing upright.
From child to adult
is evolution, too.
As we learn,
we change, alter our beliefs,
correct our errors hopefully.
What we thought we knew
when we were young
is often half the story.
There is more to learn.
Our adolescent thinking
erodes, smooths over
from the storms of living,
loving, and feeling.
We are not who we were.
Even our bodies change
as we bend with the winds of age.

GRAVITY

Gravity, gravitas, gravid, and grave—
probably the most serious things in life,
but then there is gravy,
and that upsets the connections,
although gravy has its own seriousness
whether in the making or on a necktie.
But the tie business, like the others,
happens through a downward pull.
One who is gravid brings forth life
down through the birth canal,
and on and on it goes.
We may stand tall for a little while,
but eventually we fall,
and gravity pulls us down.
Life itself, while we have it
is something else,
something special, unexpected, undeserved—
until we find the grave.

GRATITUDE

Is gratitude enough
for those of us
privileged in life?
No action of ours
brought forth that privilege.
It came by accident
randomly at birth.
Our genes gave us the wit
to make use of privilege,
to accept what came so easily.
Is gratitude enough
to keep us satisfied
with what we are?

WINNING

So many awards,
so many prizes,
medals, cups, trophies,
and even cash.
Television thrives on them
with Academy Awards winners
mostly being humble in acceptance
while the losing nominees
politely applaud for them.
Every game has winners
and losers, too.
Competition seems the goal
and winning of the most importance,
but for every winner,
there are thousands
who take pride in their work
and find satisfaction in their sport
just by doing it
and enjoying the game.

BLUE JAYS

It is easy
to forget the magnificence
of blue jays.
They are so common
and so eager
to empty the bird feeders
in the back yard.
Watch their flight
so strong,
so purposeful
and yet so everyday.
Too often we don't take notice—
just as we often
overlook our own ordinary days.

STINGING WORDS

Who taught us to say,
"Sticks and stones
can break my bones
but names will never hurt me?"
It is so truly untrue.
Stinging, hateful words can stay inside,
fester, and grow unseen
long after they are said.
Once heard,
a spoken word can linger for a lifetime,
returning again and again.

TOWN MEMORIALS

How quiet these places become
after many a year.
Few people stop to see
what the memorial's for.
When the pain was new,
people came to remember
all that was lost.
Towns erected statues
and officials made speeches
that people heard.
Now, maybe once a year
on a special day,
people come to learn
that there was a war
and some of their people were heroes
and some were lost,
but it was long ago.

PEOPLE LIKE US

People like us
rarely get into the newspapers
except for births, deaths, and marriages.
Once in a while,
if we're celebrating,
we may get stopped
by a Puritan cop and get written up,
but that could happen to anyone
and often does.
No, we don't win the lottery,
and we're not famous for anything.
We do go about our daily lives
quietly without fanfare or notice.
Yet, we do get things done.
We're the people who volunteer
to serve on committees,
deliver Meals-on-Wheels,
support churches and charities,
and go to town meetings.
We vote, pay our taxes and live peacefully
with our neighbors.
We're needed.
What could go on
if we were not here?

NUMBERS

We are ruled by numbers.
Each of us is counted
in a census in a town or city
to pay our taxes and to send each child
to school each year for a certain number of days.
Our houses are numbered,
and our cars are licensed
with colored numbers on the plates.
The hours we work
and the vacation days we take
all are counted and kept track of.
Numbers themselves are limitless,
but what they stand for
does have limits
whether in dollars, pounds,
states, sea, or fingers.
If you think of it,
even our days are numbered.

A BUTTERFLY'S WING

A butterfly's wing
is a fragile thing,
but it's been said
that the flutter of a single wing
on the other side of the world
can touch the winds
and change the weather here.
How can we believe
a butterfly has such power?
And yet, and yet,
I like believing it.
I'd like to believe, too,
that each of us, each day,
could do one kind thing
unselfishly
for all our lives
so we, together,
might amass the power
to tame the winds
and alter, then,
the coming deadly storms.

APRIL 14, 2021

This is the first year
Jack won't have a birthday.
Oh, the date came
as it always does,
but Jack's no longer here.
Others have this birthday,
and somewhere, someone new
will claim this day,
but Jack will not be here.
Do you think the dead
still remember days?
Will they know
that we remember them
particularly on the days
when their birthdays were?

LONG AFTER CHRISTMAS

After Valentine's Day,
in time for Lent,
a Christmas tree has lost its place.
It may still stand
pretending to belong
but seems unloved.
It can't have ever been alive,
or brittle branches could break off
and ornaments would scatter
as the tree drops and droops.
Tinsel will tarnish,
and dust will dim
the shine of glass and silver.
Christmas is past.
It's time to look for spring.

LEGENDS

Most legends are just people underneath.
Even The Legend of Sleepy Hollow
is Ichabod Crane and Brom Bones,
people made up in someone's imagination.
But what of the real ones
we call legends
in their time or ours?
How did they get to be that?
It can't be the case
of living a long, long time.
If it were, then that legendary woman
in the Balkans who lived to an unbelievable age
would have a name we'd know.
No, most legends had to do something special.
Johnny Appleseed planted trees,
Ella Fitzgerald and Willy Nelson sang
(though not together).
Some played sports, and some wrote music,
and all of them were always people
with loves and hates,
like all of us—
with pains and uncertainties,
like all of us.
But still, very, very few of us
will ever be called legends.

THOSE OF US

Those of us
who tend our gardens,
lead our lives for ourselves,
and do no harm
can do harm.
If we don't look beyond ourselves,
we'll never see
what could be done
in the world.
We'll never see
all that
we have left undone.

NEW SALEM

TRACKS IN THE SNOW

Whose tracks in the snow
do I see from my window?
They've crossed the neighbor's apple trees,
passed through my yard,
gone up the other neighbor's fence,
turned, and walked into the woods.
It must have been a deer
dragging its feet through the snow
and looking for some kind of food.
Do they lose heart in winter
when snow seems to cover the world?
I know, in the past,
they have stripped a young peach tree
and nibbled a shrub to the ground.
Sadly, I never replanted tree or shrub
for deer to forage in winter.
What will they feed on
here and now?
What's left for them in the snow?

A DARK DAY

What light there is
is in the snow
already on the ground.
The sky is dark
with unremitting gray
where we should see the sun.
The backyard birds
don't seem to feel the cold
but feed and feed
and scratch the snow
to pick up what
another bird has tossed away.
Then, in a flash
they disappear
and come back one by one.
One small junco
bravely hops about
knowing no importance.
His slate gray feathers
match the day, and he belongs.
Is there a lesson here?

LATE MARCH

How strange it is
to see another snow
when I had set
my heart on spring.
The signs of spring are here.
The green of daffodils
is pushing through the soil,
flocks of redwing blackbirds
surround the feeders
twice a day,
and the sun rises
too high for snow,
but here it is.
What can we do
but wait for spring
and hope that summer
doesn't come too soon?

IN MARCH

The redwings are back!
It's a sure sign of spring
even when the snow's still on the ground.
You can see the flock
scratching eagerly at seeds in the snow
after their long flight.
The black of these birds
glistens in the sun, and as they peck at the ground,
you can see the yellow stripe on the females' wings
and a red slash on the males'.
The flock rises and flies to the trees,
but some come back, one at a time.
They are a sign that says truly
that spring is near.

MAY IN NEW ENGLAND

I've put away
my winter coat
in spite of talk of frost tonight.
Is it faith or hope
or foolishness
or even common sense?
After all, it's May,
even in New England.
Maybe it's a combination,
but it's more likely
that I know
how things should be,
and May should be
beyond the frost.
If I am cold tonight,
I'll have to
put the blame
where it belongs:
on my conceit
that I know
how things should be.

THE VIEW FROM MY PORCH
JUNE 2020

There is a wind today.
It's more than a breeze—
the trees can feel it.
The new young trees bow
while the magnificent maples,
branches rich with summer leaves,
rustle and respond.
Perhaps there'll be a storm
altering the landscape
that I see this morning.
Trees are not meek,
though they will inherit the earth
when all of us are gone.
As for me, I do not know
what spins the earth.
It's not been my concern.
I do know I have had my turn
and played the game of life.

MAPLES ON THE COMMON

The trees on the common,
magnificent—
maples nearly four stories high
in full leaf now
and attentive to every breeze.
I have seen a photograph
in some archive
of the mailman in 1920,
his horse and buggy
stopped at a mailbox
near those trees, slender then.
Of course there are trees
younger than them by far,
and yet they seem
to attain the same magnificence.
What changes have there been
since first those trees were planted?
How many wars
have the townspeople seen?
How many children have played
under their branches,
and how many have seen
their own children do the same?

I cannot help but wonder
of those who have gone away
and live in different places,
do they still dream
of the trees on the common?

OLD LILACS

Old lilacs,
part of memory
(mine and unknown generations'),
still go on
as if they belonged there,
were forever there.
I have seen the blossoms
someone planted long before my time.
Emblems of New England spring,
their branches live
coated with frost and snow
through winter.
In spring, they shed all hint of frozen days
and start to leaf
and then to blossom,
deep color purple
seen in dooryards
when funeral trains passed
for great men who died.
Old lilacs,
old friends now.
live in ways they know,
keeping faith
with memory.

OVERLOOKING QUABBIN RESERVOIR

The hills that were are islands.
The valley that was is all water.
The towns that were are legend,
and the people that were are forgotten.
I go to the lookout now
on a bright October day.
Where the sun hits, the water's
a deep sapphire blue,
but where there is shade,
there's ebony. Shadows lurk
among the trees, but, too,
those trees are red and gold
amidst a palette of green pine.
It is a glorious day.
Summer's still remembered,
and no hint of winter's in the breeze.
I take in the view past the hills
and past the water,
and I see the now
with a sense of loss for what was
and a sense of joy for what is
on this October day.

OWNERSHIP

I don't know whose woods these are.
No farmer's near, nor woodsman.
Earth ought not be so parceled out
like wheels of cheese
or loaves of bread.
Instead, it should belong to all.
How arrogant a man must be
to see his name upon a deed
and walk the lines or count the stones
as if all nature were his own.
No, as far as any land's concerned,
we may choose a spot and chop some trees,
but if some day we look away,
the woods will claim the land again
as if we were not here.

I have my little acreage,
but it's not mine to keep.
It's only rented for a while,
and when I go to sleep,
some other tenant will assume
that, by a kind of right divine,
he or she can make a home
in what I thought was mine.

SEPTEMBER 1, 2020

On a path through the woods
there are last year's oak leaves
strewn across casually
with one or two green ones
come down a day or two ago
when winds were fierce.
Further on, a few red leaves
are added to the path
to remind us that fall is near
and winter's yet to come.
Still, at home, tomatoes on the vine
are not yet nearly red
and flowers not yet frosted.
It's much too soon to feel a chill
as summer lingers on.

NOVEMBER 10, 2020

What is so rare as a day in June
when it comes to us in November?
Has a sudden flap of a butterfly wing
turned the world upside down
and the Southern Hemisphere come north
to change places with its counterpart?
Scientists may tell us when they know,
when it's been studied, discussed in learned journals,
and explained to us simpler folk.
But in the meantime,
the world will do what it does
whatever we may think about it,
and if we're smart,
we'll take pleasure in the good times
whenever they come to us.

AUTUMN

How carelessly leaves fall
when trees no longer have a use for them.
Some skitter across the grass
while others, airborne,
seem like birds seeking a new tree
before they come to earth.
They nestle at the feet of parent trees
or crowd against stone walls
and at last carpet all the grass.
The summer season's over.
It's time to stack the wood,
bring house plants indoors,
and hunker down for winter.
Everything changes with the seasons,
and carefully we must prepare
for winter's sure to come.
We button up our houses,
put outside tools away,
and hope we've not forgotten one.
It's time to come inside
where it is warm
and supper's waiting.

CATS AND DOGS

NELLIE

At my house, there is a cat
always needy, never satisfied.
To pet her once
begins her expectations.
Her claws extend,
and she kneads,
leaving pinholes bleeding on my knees.
To brush her is to look at ecstasy
almost embarrassing.
When you leave her,
her forgiveness is palpable.
She turns her back
and curls her front paws neatly under her
and waits so patiently, so earnestly
for you to do again
whatever it is you do
that is never enough.

HOPE

My little dog
who's growing old now
sleeps through the night
with little yips
as if she feels some pain.
Of course, she may be dreaming
that she's chasing squirrels
or running joyfully with friends.

I, too, am old now,
so when I feel little pains,
perhaps I'll tell myself
that I am dreaming
so I can run
joyously with friends.
At least, I have that hope.

AGGIE

I can feel my cat's livingness
when she's on my lap
allowing me to pet her.
She stretches and retracts her paws and claws
and burrows her head
into my elbow bend
and pushes, purring, against me,
her eyes closed in bliss.
She knows she is an important cat,
a cat who's loved and loves herself.
What a lesson for us all.

WISDOM

I'm sure my cat has mastered
the meaning of life.
She sleeps for hours at a time
secure in her wisdom.
My dog doesn't care.
She takes each day as it comes
without concern for any cat's wisdom.

PERSONAL

LIFE

When I was young,
often I'd speak of LIFE,
all letters capitalized,
as if it were not then
but someplace in the future.
As I grew older,
it became someplace else,
but now that I am old,
I know that it is here,
in this place, for me.
No longer in capitals,
but safe in lower case
for as long as I will see it.

OLD HOUSES

Those of us who live
in old houses
do sometimes feel the spirit
of those who lived here before.
I don't mean ghosts or wraiths.
No eerie thing appears in the night.
It's more a sense of love they've left behind.
I see it in the daffodils
they planted in their time,
which bloom with those I planted in mine.
From cellar to attic,
we share a link,
a feeling of contentment.
It's not that the house
belongs to any of us
but that we belong in this place.
Now I hope
that I will add a link
to the loving spirit of this house
for those who follow me.

PROTECTED

When I was a child,
it never crossed my mind
the world could be a hostile place.
I was well protected.
Though born in the midst of the Depression,
I never noticed it.
There was a cast iron stove in the kitchen.
It kept us warm and well fed.
Then there was a war
which didn't affect me
except we had a name for the enemy
in schoolyard games.

Should I have seen beyond my years?
What could I have noticed?

SPEAKING OUT

My voice in this wilderness
is too calm, too soft
for any but my own ears to hear.
Why am I not
on the streets
shouting to be heard?
Have I grown too soft,
too comfortable to take the risk
of looking a little foolish?

EGO

The child I once was
still lives within me
rushing to resent
when I am slighted or patronized
or, even worse, ignored.
Now that my hair is white
and my step slowed,
I have learned somewhat to curb
the temper of that spoiled child
whom I named Ego.
If I look for wisdom,
I can't complain
even when it doesn't come.
I have had a good life
and continue to have it,
for I have found joy
in laughter,
sunny days,
and loving friends.

CHOICES

How much of the me that is
has been of my choosing?
The parents who loved me,
though they had their problems,
gave me the color of my eyes,
my hair, my skin.
Most of my life
has been a reaction
to all that and more.
Did I choose to grow old,
to lose track of what I read
and have to read it again?
Old age may limit me,
but still I have the choice
of how I love
other people
and the life I live.

MY TURN

Did someone take my place in line,
leaving me to stay longer?
I can only hope it was someone
willing to go, willing for an end
to whatever their life had become.
It would be ironic
if that someone were young
and sad if the person wanted more.
I know we all die,
some too soon while
others like me can go on and on
until we take our turns.

WHAT AM I OWED?

What am I owed in this world?
A living? True love? No,
they must be earned.
Respect would be nice,
but I, myself, cannot respect
the bigoted, the cruel,
the hateful, or those
who are self-righteous,
and I have my doubts
that they would offer me respect.
Kindness given or taken
enriches me,
but to my knowledge,
it is not owed nor even earned.
No, all I can think
that what is owed to me
is common courtesy.
Equally, I owe it to the world.

SHARING THE WORLD

No matter how I see myself
or what I call myself,
I am one of many.
I may be a woman, sister,
aunt, or citizen of America,
and my hair may be white,
but there are many
who say the same.
I may be myself,
and yet I share the world
with others who are like me
in one way or another.
I doubt I've ever had a thought
that someone else hasn't thought as well
or will consider some time or another.
Although we like to think ourselves
as different, set apart somehow,
we are so alike, all of us,
that we ought not
to make so much of differences.

EACH MORNING

Each morning when I wake,
I stay a bit in bed
to gather my wits about me
and make sure my limbs still move.
Then I get up to see the sun.
I rise with it quite early
and do the must-do things of morning.
A ritual—dog out and dog in,
dog fed, cats fed,
coffee brewing, make the bed.
Shower and dress at last,
then scan the paper
to see if the world's still there.
I try not to be afraid
or give in to despair
for what I know is happening
somewhere.
My little corner still is safe.
The threats seem far away,
but it may not be long now
for the world to change.
It will not, it seems,
end with fire and ice.
The ice is melting,
but the fires are there,
not everywhere,
but growing closer year by year.

WHAT I WANT

Now that I am old,
sometimes I am asked what I want
when I shake off this mortal coil.
It is always a solemn moment
for those asking.
I don't like being fussed over now,
so don't assume I want it then.
No fuss. No bother.
Let me go simply in a cardboard box
with no audience except a paid one.
Then put my ashes anywhere.
Preferably in the yard
where they'll mix with the earth I loved.

DEATH

Death has no face.
It's not a he, not a person,
just a state of being
or not being.
One day you're here,
and then you no longer are.
The metaphors of a scythe and hooded figure
are not reality. Never were.
Charon won't guide you across the River Styx,
but perhaps, as Edith Wharton once wished,
you'll be met joyfully by every dog
you ever loved, and I'd include
those many cats we've taken to our hearts.

THINGS

When I look around my house,
in my mind
I see names attached to things
like the magic lantern slide resting on a windowsill.
I gave that to Janet Soyer,
but she gave it back to me
when she knew she was dying.
Then there's the portrait of a woman
painted by Dorothy Cogswell.
I bought it from her
among other things
when she was leaving South Hadley.
She had painted it in the thirties.
Then there are the watercolors Leonard Baskin
gave us on birthdays always signed to Doris and Dorothy
no matter whose birthday it was.
There's a Staffordshire elephant
on a kitchen shelf.
It has my father's name on it.
I bought it at a tag sale
but gave it to him for Father's Day
years and years ago.
It's with me now.
There are things
with names on them
in my mind all over my house.
Of course the things will go on
to someone else, even somewhere else.
Maybe they'll know my name,
but will it matter to me then
when other names are forgotten?

MEMORIES

My life has been a long one.
Memories are kept in an old trunk
in the attic.
From time to time,
I take one out
to polish and enjoy.
A thousand hurts are rolled up
like a ball of string.
I don't remember who or why,
but I can see a pattern there
that gives me something to think about.
In spring, I think about things I treasure.
I take them down from shelves,
wash and put them back again.
Old dust can dull bright things.
Occasionally I may give away
some treasure so that others
may find joy in them.
It's good to know
when it's time to give away.
I cannot only look at yesterday—
today is here and now,
and there is much still undone.

THE SELF

Of course, I know my birth date.
I have celebrated it every year
for years and years,
but I cannot remember
just when I began.
We all have the Self inside,
but I don't know when I became aware of it.
Was it there when I was a fat newborn,
and I just took it for granted
until one day I noticed I had a Self?
Or did it appear one day
out of the blue?
Are there Selves in the ether
waiting to find a newborn to settle into?
It's a curious question I ask myself as I grow older.
Has my Self grown older, too? Maybe a little wiser?
Gertrude Stein said that we are always the same age inside.
I'm sure that's not quite accurate.
I think it's more likely that we are ageless inside,
for whatever difference that makes to a Self.

WRITING A POEM

I cannot force a poem
like an amaryllis
in a pot. I cannot put it in the sun,
water it, and watch it grow.
It is. or it isn't.
Let it find its path
and wind its way
to meaning.
If I try to push it
one way or another,
it will stand there awkward
like a schoolboy reciting,
hoping to finish soon.
It will just be words
and no poem at all.

MY CONCEPT OF TIME

My concept of time
is so confusing
that I doubt it's mine alone.
In childhood, days were long,
and time between birthdays
seemed to go on forever.
Perhaps it was because
everything was new then.
When I grew up,
I had no time for time,
but now,
close to the end
of my eighties,
the days slip by.
Time is in a hurry now.
I cannot slow it down.
How curious it is
that each year has
the same number of days,
the days the same in hours,
the hours in minutes—
but our perceptions differ.

TWO POEMS

I lost two poems today.
I had them
almost in my grasp,
and they darted away
like tiny fish
in a big pond.
Perhaps they were not real—
only figments
in my imagination.
Should they return,
I might not know them
because they have
become real.

THE NEIGHBORS' GRANDCHILD

What was she
before she was Cassie,
five years old and full of life?
She had to have been something,
something of substance.
All that energy had to have existed
all along. Somewhere.

LIMITATIONS

I cannot walk a mile
in shoes of yours.
Too small, too big
it matters not,
your shoes will never fit
and should I try
I know they'll break my stride
and cripple me.
Instead, let me walk with you
side by side
each in our own shoes.

I cannot know your life.
It is not mine.
Too soft, too harsh
I hear your words
but I can't take your pain from you.
I know I must speak
though I know it will not change the world.
I am only me
just one small voice
in a nation of noise
but still I have to speak
or every hope is gone.

THIS DAY

My special time
is this day.
How extraordinary
that this old self
is able to rise up out of bed,
feed the dog and cats,
and make my coffee.
How grand it is
to sit and look
out a window
and see the rain.

THE INEVITABLE

Each day moves us
closer to the inevitable,
and when that comes for me,
I shall not ask for nor expect
stones with my name on them.
Too often we try
saving ourselves
with monuments
as if we are still here.
No, my ashes will mix with soil.
In time, much will be gone.
No matter what we want in the far future,
mountains will erode,
and even Niagara Falls
will be a quiet stream
if it exists at all.
Then and only then I hope
the spark that was humanity
will light a path
for whatever comes next,
wherever it may be.

TIME

Time...
We are able to
keep it, mark it, learn to tell it,
take ours and yours or even theirs,
pass it, kill it, serve it, and even lose track of it
as if we are in control.
Did we think we created it
by making calendars and clocks?
We are aware of the changes in the moon
its slenderness and fullness
and we know our planet does revolve
around the sun and not the other way,
but when did time itself come into our awareness?
When I wake in the morning
I see the clock, but I am more
aware of the minute of waking, stretching,
and getting out of bed.
That same minute someone in another state
unknown to me
may be tending a restless child in the night.
We share that minute but it's a different time.
Even more confusing, my minute shared
by anyone in a different hemisphere
may find a different day.
It matters little
whether we keep it or spend it,
time goes on without
concern for watch or calendar
or any earthly things
much like infinity
and probably eternity.

IN THIS MOMENT

Even as I live and breathe
in this particular moment,
things are going on outside myself,
things that I can only guess
or let myself imagine
to people I don't know.
As I drink my coffee,
someone somewhere's hard at work
and someone else is swimming in a pool.
Farther away, a man tries on a pair of shoes,
while in another place, a woman shovels snow.
We speak of a small world,
but millions of people of all races,
classes, sizes, shapes, and ages
live and breathe at the same time
even when we think ourselves alone.

AGE

The accumulation of years
has slowed my steps.
I don't think I could run,
and I take stairs one by one.
But still . . .
I am still here
though my hearing fails.
I'm still the same inside
though that self, too, has changed.
I like to think I've grown,
that I have found some wisdom.
Finally.

CONFESSION

I have always thought of myself
as a strong person.
Of course, I have had my weaknesses,
but I could live with them.
Now I know that it was vanity.
I liked to think well of myself.
As I am ending my eighty-seventh year,
I know my weaknesses better
because more and more
they have become visible.
I am conscious
when I forget a word or name
or when I take too long
to get out of a chair
and other people are around.
I think I can see them thinking,
"Oh, oh, Dorothy is failing,"
and I am ashamed—
not so much of my weakness,
for I have begun to accept it,
but of my vanity—
which seems a greater failing.

TEARS

I have no idea how many
tears I've shed
during my many years.
I know I cry every time
I read in Dickens books
and Little Nell dies or Jo.
I've swallowed tears in movies and plays
when the sad part comes,
and I try hard not to sob aloud,
but I suspect those tears are cheap,
brought on by sentiment.
Of course, I weep at funerals,
but happy endings, too, can choke me up.
In spite of easy tears,
I have known sorrow
more than once,
and those tears cost me dearly.
But there's not been a tear
that I regret.
Never a one was wasted
nor were any smiles,
given or received.
Laughter has been cherished,
'though I can't seem to recollect
the times when laughter came.
There were so many.

NOSTALGIA

When I drive past
the places I've lived,
I remember other houses I visited
there and over there.
I remember what the kitchens were like
or what they were like long ago.
I played in that yard and went to parties there,
but much has changed,
The houses are strangers to me now,
gilded with memory
but not known to me.
And the people of my past—
so many gone now.
I can't always remember names
or put their faces in my mind.
I hope someone thinks of them
remembering names and faces
more fully than I do the days
when I was young.

ANYTHING IMPORTANT

Do you remember when,
as a child, you first discovered your teacher was a real person?
She maybe chewed gum
or drove a car.
Perhaps she went to a movie,
and you saw her eating popcorn.
Remember that?
Did you ever see
a celebrity in person?
I know I read about
movie stars in the magazines.
They lived in Hollywood
and could lounge by their swimming pools.
That was glamour. That was high living.
Maybe you wished that,
for convertibles and suntans in January—
maybe even a chauffeur
just for one day, maybe,
just to see what it was like.
Of course, that never happens,
not in real life,
but I don't think
I missed out
on anything important.
Did you?

THEN AND NOW

When I try to see myself as a young woman,
I never see my face.
I am usually walking with purpose
down a New York street,
going to work in a dress—
wearing high heels.
If I could see my face,
I know I'd be wearing lipstick.
Occasionally, I can see myself
at an office desk
with a stack of papers in front of me.
Much has changed.
New York has gone,
'though I know it still is there—
I am here.
For years I have lived in a small village.
Now, through my kitchen window,
I watch others walk by.
They seem so swift and sure.
My walk would be too slow for them.

A FANTASY

If I had one chance
to dial up the dead,
who would I telephone?
I should not dare to call any
of the illustrious gone so long ago.
Shakespeare, Dickens, Dickinson
have already given their words.
It would be greedy to ask for more.
I doubt I'd call on those closest to me.
What if they'd already moved on
and no longer remembered me?
The hurt would be too great.
Perhaps I'd call up ones I knew just enough
to be at ease asking what death was like.
Would they be able to tell me
and could I understand?
Would there be language shared
or just an awareness?
Everything now is a question,
but I have faith the answers
will come in their own time—
not too soon, not too early or late,
but in a time that I could understand.
Until then, I'll wait.

OLD AGE

If old age hadn't found me,
who knows what I could do
except for some new weaknesses
beyond the ones I knew?
Perhaps I'd climb a mountain
or write a poem or two,
but legs don't move the way they should
and words I know can disappear
even while I'm thinking them
and many voices I can't hear.
But, still, I see the sun come up.
I'm grateful in my way
and hope I'll make the best of it
and do some good today.

THE HEREAFTER

I'm well aware of the Here.
It's the After that eludes me.
I doubt that anyone expects
angels in white robes singing
for eternity. No, eternity
and infinity are twin forevers.
Perhaps, then, it makes sense
for whatever spirit, soul, or energy—
call it what you will—
to flow eternally
into infinite space, to become one with it.
I may know soon,
but, then again, energy itself is unknowing,
so I'll be forever unaware.

MILESTONES

I know people who fear death,
yet it seems to me
just another milestone to get through
like childhood or growing up.
Life's a lot like housework—
never quite all done.
There's always another floor to sweep,
another dish to wash,
and there are always cobwebs,
but I can't envision you or me
cleaning for eternity.
Often I've been present
when people I have loved have died,
and when that final breath has gone
only the living noticed.
What seems hard to me for now
is that I'll never know
how children of the ones I've known
turn out to be like in the end
and what the world will look like then
when I have ceased to be.

A DEATH IN THE HOUSE

How busy we are
when there's a death in the house.
So much to do—
people to tell,
people to see,
finding the words
to convey our loss
without being a burden to others.
So much detail to take care of—
paying leftover bills
and clearing out whatever's left.
There are days and days
when there's no time to grieve,
but then comes the day
when silence descends
and only our footsteps
are heard in the house.

OLD MEMORIES

Did I know love?
Of course I did,
and passions bursting forth
and all the messy sex
that went with that.
Now, remembering that joy and pain,
I'm just as glad
that memories
alone
remain.

ENLIGHTENMENT

In the night
when I look out my window,
I can see shapes outside—
trees and moving animals,
if animals be there.
When I turn on a light,
I see my room
but no shadows.
Windows are black boxes
reflecting the room within.
Is all my vision skewed
by lights within the house
until the sun comes up?

REMEMBRANCES

I would expect
no mournful cries
when I am gone
because
I've been
so long about it.
Rather, I hope
that some small kindness
I forgot
might be remembered.
It need not have
my name about it.
The kindness is
what is important.

2020
POLITICS AND PANDEMIC

VIRUS 2020

They may be nameless now,
but we know the dead.
We have seen pictures
of their white-covered bodies
stacked silently waiting to disappear.
Even though the winds of virus
have not whistled through
our acquaintance,
we know the dead.
They are grandfathers and uncles,
old soldiers,
doctors and musicians,
aunts and married cousins,
nurses and doormen.
They have delivered furniture
and babies to us.
They've taken our credit cards
and filled our cars with gasoline.
All those whom we have known
but never knew their names—
they are us
and so we mourn.

ANOTHER WEEK

Another week has passed—
a week closer to something
and farther from something else.
Hard to define,
to know which way to look,
to take a step
and know just where you're going.
I scarcely know what I have done
in the week that's passed.
Days are filled with thoughts,
my own and other people's
in whatever I am reading.
How long they'll stay with me
I cannot say.
These days, each one
so like the last
and probably the next
because of a pandemic,
add up to a week—
another week that's gone.

2020

There are good years
and bad years
but this year, this 2020
has been the most uncertain,
the most isolating and enervating.
We wait for good news,
but it doesn't come uncluttered.
First it was the pandemic,
then the distraction
of the election.
Although I'm pleased
with the promised changes to come,
I'm not ready to cheer.
I can't foresee what else is coming with them.
I do know I'm grateful
to be an old woman.

QUARANTINED AT HOME
JULY 2020

Each day is like the next
and like the day before.
It's hard to know the date
unless I see a calendar.
Monday slides to Thursday
without a qualm.
Friday and Sunday
maintain the calm.
Other days there are, of course,
but matter not at all.
One day I wash my clothes,
and each day sweep the floor,
make some meals, walk the dog,
but I am never sure
which day is which.

ENDURING THE PANDEMIC

I have been told
that, in the city,
people stand in the streets
or at their windows
and shout out "Thank you"
to all those others
who are working still—
to the doctors,
bankers, grocery clerks,
pharmacists, and public servants
who help the rest of us
to get through
the strange isolation
the virus has brought.
I know they deserve thanks,
but then I thought
how many thanks are due from me
for all the years I've known.
As a person, I owe thanks
to teachers, friends, and family, of course.
As a reader, I owe thanks
to authors past and present—
sometimes for volumes and
sometimes for a single sentence
in a single book.
It's a non-ending list
and will go on
for as long as I am here.

THE GOOD GERMANS

We are the good Germans
of this generation
keeping busy with our everyday concerns,
waiting for someone to guide us.
We keep our kitchens warm
and our yards clean.
The grass is mowed neatly in straight lines
while we wait for someone to guide us,
to give our lives meaning.

JUST WAR

Is there a just war
or is it just a war?
Word placement matters little
when there's killing to be done.

WHO ARE WE?

Who are the we
we speak of
when we say "We Americans"?
Do we include the people
who were here
when the Europeans arrived?
What about the hyphenated ones?
Do they count,
the Italian-Americans, the African-Americans,
and all the others
from all over the world?
Do they count?
Do we all speak
the same language,
hold dear the same mythologies?

How can we define ourselves
when we are so many,
when we see only differences?
If we are the people,
who can say who we are?

A SILENT VIGIL
ORANGE MASSACHUSETTS

On a Saturday morning,
some few of us stand in the line
at the edge of the Orange Peace Park.
We are silently holding signs
and staring at a brick building.
Though an outside hanging sign says Ames Trophy,
the front door says "no trespassing."
The building is old,
bearing witness to Orange's history.
We can still read in the faded paint
that it once was the New Home Sewing . . .
and a floor below adds Needle.
That was back when Orange was a prosperous town.
I asked myself that day,
"Why am I standing here
holding a sign that says Women in Black?"
Others hold a banner that speaks of justice,
and another sign says War Is Not the Answer.
I can believe in these things,
but there is little hope
that this small group of people
will ever influence anyone else.
There is so much wrong.
We build walls that keep us in
and others out.
No place is left for those once welcomed—
none for the huddled masses yearning to breathe free.
Do we ourselves breathe free
with cameras on many corners
and telephones ringing with scams
and so many guns in so many hands?
It's overwhelming.

A WORRY

How will I know
where to stand
if I have never stood before
to be counted?
Who will tell me,
or will I be marched
threadbare to wherever
some guard points?
I hope I will know
how to be brave
when I have never been brave before.

THE SHIP OF STATE

Our ship of state seems
to have turned into the *Pequod*
with Ahab at the helm
seeking revenge against a whale.
Can I believe the people chose
this Ahab for their captain
as again and again
he trumpets the errors of his ways?
What will become of this, our nation?
Can we find the greatness
we assumed was ours by right?
The possibility is always there,
almost within our reach,
if only, if only . . .

FOR DONALD TRUMP

A liar will not know the truth.
If he sees a lake
and calls it an ocean
twice or thrice,
he will believe it ocean
despite no evidence of salt.

CONTROL

Was there someone in control
when Nero fiddled?
Who decided the
everyday concerns of the people?
Was there one senator or several
who applauded the song
while running the world
as they knew it?

THEY

How dare they change our world?
Didn't they know
it was good the way it was,
the way we liked it?
But no, they couldn't leave well enough alone.
They needed more, more, and more,
and now the ice cap is melting.
They've changed the winds,
and storms batter our shores.
Fires burn the land where fires never were.
I suppose we have to take some blame.
After all, we let it happen.
No doubt some eccentrics warned of this,
but who believes a man
who doesn't live in the real world
and work like a real man?
Will they ever hear our voices
raised, asking them to stop?
How can they?
It's not likely,
because they are us
and we are them.

THE STATUE OF LIBERTY

The times of crisis when we speak
so hopefully of our imperfect union,
I am reminded of our statue
who bears the words,
"Give me your tired, your poor,
your huddled masses . . . "
I know the words are meant for immigrants,
for those coming into this country
for better things in life.
I question, then,
to whom does she speak?
Does she speak those words
including all races seeking freedom?
She stands in New York Harbor,
but perhaps she should look beyond
and see deep into our country.
The irony should not be lost.

SHEPHERDS

If there be shepherds,
let them come now
while wildfires set the stars ablaze
and the seas rise,
perhaps to meet the fires.
The wise men will be late again,
stepping carefully over the hot sand
afraid to fall, afraid to fail,
stopping now and then
to collect a tax
or see if their investments prosper.
We need a shepherd now
to save the flock from wolves
and keep the new lambs safe.

TIME TO SPEAK

A little wisdom
goes a long, long way.
There is a time for silence
and a time to speak,
but silence is complicit
when guns speak for us.
Whatever hope there is
dies when the guns are heard.

MYTHOLOGY

TITHONUS

Once upon a time
when myths were new,
Aurora asked the gods
to make her husband, Tithonus, immortal.
Even the gods could deny the dawn nothing,
but she forgot to ask for youth for him.
He could not die
but grew older and older
and smaller than life.
Now, when a thought
seems to come
out of the air
and seems to be everywhere
at once,
perhaps it is Tithonus
sharing a whisper
on the wind.

It is as reasonable
an explanation
for an idea
as any.

THE FLOOD

How did Noah decide
which animals to take with him
or was it known
before they came
two by two?
And anyway,
what had the other animals done
that they should perish in the flood?
It's easy to understand
that mankind's errors
brought about destruction.
We have done it more than once
and continue to do it now.

SHEEP

We are but sheep
waiting for someone to take care of us.
Noah keeps busy with his building,
and his wife knits our wool
to keep her family warm
while we wait
shivering in the rain.

DISTANT THUNDER

The rumble of distant thunder
is no threat.
It cannot touch us.
Close by, a thunderous clap
can startle our bones,
but it is only noise.
All power is in the lightning.
It can electrify and burn,
scorching trees and bodies,
devastating forests and houses.
Small wonder the ancients
found a Being
who could hold the lightning bolts,
though he himself
had, oh, such human traits.

SOME THOUGHTS

As a child,
I had forever before me,
but in age,
forever closes in.
Life itself seems ephemeral.
What is it after all?
A breath, a thought, a whisper?
Those who are alive now
live in the midst of ghosts
who've lived before.
The oak I see now
was an acorn
forgotten by a squirrel generations ago.
The maples on the common ground
were set a century ago
by those who governed here.
Even the house I live in now
has known so many others.
My steps retrace their steps
as those who will come after
will follow mine unknowing.

Dorothy Johnson

ABOUT THE AUTHOR

Playwright and poet Dorothy Johnson has regaled, captivated, and challenged many audiences over the years.

Resident of New Salem, Massachusetts, since 1971, Dorothy operated the Common Reader Bookshop there with her partner, Doris Abramson, until their retirement in 2000. Long a bibliophile, she worked with MacMillan publisher in New York City in the 1950s and has, among much wider reading, encountered all of Dickens several times over.

She wrote the script and lyrics for musical comedies she directed for New Salem's 1794 Meetinghouse. Composers Andrew Lichtenberg and Steven Schoenberg provided the music. A hallmark of her playwriting oeuvre involves capitalizing on the idiosyncrasies of players mimicking themselves to comic effect.

Known for her pungent quick wit and humble, decent heart, Dorothy grew up in South Hadley, Massachusetts, where she was born in 1933. Her family left a rented farm in Enfield, Massachusetts, one of the towns drowned to make way for Quabbin Reservoir to serve Greater Boston.

Dorothy attended public schools through ninth grade, when she went to Macduffie School for Girls in Springfield, Massachusetts, where she graduated in 1950. She holds a BA in English from Mount Holyoke College in South Hadley and an MA in theatre from Smith College in Northampton.

Her work experience, she says with understatement, has involved office work in New York City, shelving books in a library, selling hamburgers, hawking antiques, purveying gift shop merchandise, offering used and sometimes rare books, and teaching at Holyoke Community College and Xavier University in New Orleans.

Dorothy began writing the poems in *My Heart Remembers* with "Shepherds" in 2019.

She writes the "Quiet Places" column for *Uniquely Quabbin* magazine.

COLOPHON

Text for *My Heart Remembers* is set in Garamond, a group of many serif typefaces named for sixteenth-century Parisian engraver Claude Garamond, generally spelled as Garamont in his lifetime. Garamond-style typefaces are popular and particularly often used for book printing and body text.

Garamond's types followed the model of an influential typeface cut for Venetian printer Aldus Manutius by his punchcutter Francesco Griffo in 1495 and are in what is now called the old-style of serif letter design, letters with a relatively organic structure resembling handwriting with a pen but with a slightly more structured, upright design.

Titles for *My Heart Remembers* are set in ITC Stone Sans, a modern version of the humanistic sans serif font reminiscent of such faces like Gill Sans, Kabel, and Syntax. The design has a moderate but visible contrast in stroke weight, large x-height, and slightly condensed proportions. The fonts are very legible and create a modern, dynamic impression.